Ideas that Work for Children with
Sensory Integration Disorders and Their Difficult Behaviors

by

Kathryn Phillips M.A.

Library of Congress
Copyright 2007

Phillips, Kathryn
  Ideas that Work for Children with Sensory Integration Disorders and Their
  Difficult Behaviors

Total Behavior Management
  A division of Phillips Associates, LLC.

ISBN 0-9776218-6-3

The environment is the extended body. It must be peaceful.

Deepak Chopra

To Robert

With love for all of his quirks

TABLE OF CONTENTS

We all use our senses to pick up information that is then translated to the brain for processing information into meaning. Our senses help us to understand the world, assist us in learning and create a foundation upon which to build new learning. Young children are even more dependent than adults on their senses to gather information from their environment since they lack brain pathways already established to support new learning. When the message from our senses is misinterpreted by the brain or ineffective in translating it to meaning, simple actions in every day life become a constant challenge of new experiences – some frightening, some annoying and some very distracting. When the world is such a confusing place for these children, behaviors such as non-compliance, defiance, refusals, hyperactivity and "lack of motivation" become commonplace. These children can have difficulties being redirected and transitioning, with "incidental learning" and have poor social skills that can seriously effect their functioning in school. It makes for a puzzling and frustrating situation for teachers, parents and the children themselves. Sensory integration and processing disorders are often linked with other developmental disorders or health conditions, such as Autism Spectrum Disorder, Fetal Alcohol Syndrome, Attention Deficit Disorder, and Oppositional Defiance Disorder as well as emotional and behavioral conditions.

This manual is intended to help guide you in identifying, understanding and addressing the behavioral and learning challenges presented by children who have sensory processing disorders. With practical, ready-to-use, research-tested interventions, this manual offers you dozens of activities, skill builders and adaptations that you can implement immediately. You will have the opportunity to use a five-step process for solving sensory-induced behaviors that was developed and field-tested by teachers such as yourself. You will learn a myriad of ideas for helping children to learn life-long strategies for self-regulation. You will gain an understanding of the connection between sensory processing issues, environmental, teaching and scheduling components for developing activities that help children integrate sensory information effectively.

Children who are sensory-sensitive are not trying to be difficult, disobedient or oppositional. They are desperately trying to make meaning from a bombardment of sensory information that is confusing, exhausting and frightening. Our job as educators is to help them to regulate their behaviors so that they can be alert, attentive and involved.

In this book you will

- ✓ Develop an understanding of sensory processing disorders and how they manifest in problematic behaviors in the classroom.

- ✓ Be able to identify the key stressors that escalate out-of-control and off-task behavior.

- ✓ Be able to apply proven strategies to help your students become aware of their own triggers and react in more productive ways.

- ✓ Learn to implement new teaching strategies that work for the sensory sensitive student.

- ✓ Use a five-step approach for systematically preventing behaviors, teaching replacement behaviors and reviewing progress.

- ✓ Add to your teacher toolkit for developing and adapting lessons for your students who exhibit volatility, poor social skills, explosive behaviors, and learning problems brought on by sensory integration problems.

- ✓ Utilize best practices for using adaptive equipment and creating environmental modifications.

- ✓ Understand the differences and similarities with look-alike conditions such as ASD, FASD, ADHD and Oppositional Defiance Disorder

- ✓ Learn new strategies for working with the three types of sensory conditions: over sensitive, under sensitive and the inability to integrate sensory information effectively.

- ✓ Create an adaptive classroom that meets the needs of all learners.

- ✓ Build on proven teaching strategies to develop sensory-based activities and learning centers.

Guiding Principles

FOR WORKING WITH CHILDREN WHO HAVE SENSORY-INDUCED PROBLEMATIC BEHAVIORS

Paradigm shift must precede behavioral change for lasting results.

Teachers have a responsibility to respond to the needs of all learners.

All behavior is an attempt to communicate something.

Children who have sensory processing issues are not deliberately trying to be difficult.

When confronted with stress, human beings typically respond in a survival mentality (fight or flight).

Children who have sensory processing issues are in a constant survival mode.

Environmental considerations, teaching styles and scheduling adaptations can be made that support the sensory sensitive child.

Adapting the environment, teaching style and scheduling does not single out a student, "water down" the experience or make the lesson any less valuable.

Making changes within the setting will help the sensory sensitive child to function at his or her optimal level.

It is the teacher's responsibility to help the sensory sensitive child to learn lifelong skills in self-regulation so that he can be attentive, on-task and ready to learn.

Equal treatment does not mean giving the same thing to everyone.

We all have our quirks.

Sensory Integration is the organization of senses for use. It is the brain's ability to filter and process incoming information from all of the senses to make meaning out of the world and react appropriately.

"Sensory Integration Dysfunction is a common, but misunderstood, problem which affects children's behavior, influencing the way they learn, move, relate to others and feel about themselves."

Carol Stock Kranowitz
Author of *"The Out of Sync Child"*

Speaking of Quirks . . .

DO you

Feel that you are more sensitive to pain than others?

Feel excessively bothered by seams in your socks and tags in your clothing?

Prefer to touch rather than be touched?

Feel very unsettled in getting your hands messy?

Feel very uncomfortable with personal care tasks such as clipping your nails or brushing your teeth?

Get terrified of heights or movement?

Feel OVERLY sensitive to sounds?

Have a strong emotional reaction to certain smells that bring back significant memories for you?

Have a difficult time reading a recipe because every time you look away you completely lose your place?

Require all of your food to be very spicy, heavily salted or at a certain temperature?

WE ALL HAVE QUIRKS. IT IS WHEN THEY INTERFERE SIGNIFICANTLY WITH THE QUALITY OF LIFE THAT IT BECOMES A PROBLEM.

HOW DO YOU COPE/COMPENSATE?

Review this sensory motor preference checklist. Think about what you do nearly instinctively to manage the stimulation in your environment. Notice which of these actions are comforting to you and which arouse your central nervous system. Circle A if the action makes you more alert and C if it calms you.

C A   Sucking on hard candy   C A   Rocking in a rocking chair

C A   Crunching on ice   C A   Aerobic exercise

C A   Chewing gum   C A   Roll neck and head slowly

C A   Tapping a pen or pencil   C A   Watching a fireplace

C A   Smoking cigarettes   C A   Drinking a carbonated drink

C A   Working with music on   C A   Sit with crossed leg and bounce it slightly

C A   Taking slow deep breaths   C A   Eating a cold popsicle

C A   Listening to classic music   C A   Listening to jazz

C A   Squirming in a chair   C A   Gently rub shoulders or skin

C A   Drumming fingers on table   C A   Receiving a massage

C A   Twisting your hair   C A   Fidgeting with paperclips, nails

C A   Watching a fish tank   C A   Taking a cool shower

C A   Walking briskly   C A   Having sunlight in the room when sleeping

C A   Tidy up a cluttered space   C A   Singing or talking to yourself

C A   Listening to baby babbling   C A   Watching a ceiling fan

C A   Hearing a squeaky door   C A   Rolling your neck or shoulders

HABITUATE SCHAMITUATE

We all have sensory preferences that are unique and personal. How you interpret a smell or taste may be very different than how someone else interprets it. Studies have shown that when questioning eyewitnesses of accidents, each person has a decidedly different perception of the experience, although each person is "telling the truth." How our bodies and minds select and perceive the visual, auditory, tactile and kinesthetic elements of the experience is very individualized. If we paid attention to all the information that was involved in the experience it would make us crazy. Most us can live in a world full of sensory bombardment only because we have learned the process called "habituation."

Habituation is the ability to sort out and ignore irrelevant stimuli so that we can attend to relevant information. For instance, there are lots of stimuli going on in your environment right now, if you stop to think about it. The ticking of clock, the hum of the computer, the feel of your backside on the chair, the taste that the onions on your burger from lunch left in your mouth (although your neighbor may not have forgotten the onions on the burger you had for lunch, you have). Your brain has learned to ignore that other stuff and listen to the speaker, or read the words on this page without getting distracted by all that other irrelevant information that is present in your environment. Habituation, it's a beautiful thing. Another thing that you have learned to do is COMPENSATE or self-regulate your behavior so that you do not become too agitated or overwhelmed even by those things than CAN bug the ba-gee-bees out of you if given half a chance. Pretty cool, huh?

Of course there are times in our lives when we are more susceptible to sensory overload than others. When we are tired, ill or stressed, for example, we are less tolerant of the sensory stimuli in our environment. Imagine feeling constantly OVER-stimulated and feeling like you must escape EVERY situation at the first opportunity. Or, if you cannot escape, you scream to get the noise, confusion, touch, or smell to stop! Or imagine that you are constantly UNDER-stimulated and you are always looking for ways to become more aroused so that you can pay attention. Being unable to habituate and compensate would be disastrous if you faced this on a moment-to-moment basis. What if you were more focused on the raindrops on the windshield than the road ahead when you were driving during a rain shower? Habituating to the environment (not hearing or seeing the raindrops, the slapping of the wipers, the dampness of the air on your skin, the smell of the ozone released in the rainfall) allows you to concentrate on driving. Good thing, huh?

The older you get, the more pathways you have in your brain that allow you to filter out irrelevant information and compensate for the stress. When you are young, you have only a few ways to deal with all that STUFF coming at you in this VERY stimulating world. Babies cry to escape, get something, stimulate themselves or to have someone pay attention to their needs. As you get older you don't cry (as much) when you must have your needs met or are struggling to deal with the environmental stimuli. When overwhelmed, we can take a walk or listen to music. When needing to be aroused, we can drink coffee, get up and move, or chew gum because we know that these things have worked for us in the past. We have LOTS of pathways and coping devices to help us get aroused to pay attention or to calm ourselves when we feel over-stimulated. Young children, and particularly those who have sensory integration difficulties, don't have those pathways, so their behavior becomes what we call "difficult," oppositional or resistant. Actually, these behaviors are really a gallant effort to have their needs met.

Of course, the more practice you have at habituating and compensating, the better you will become at it. If you only read in an environment that is completely quiet, you will have a difficult time concentrating in an airport, right? It is good to learn to read in many environments so that when the need arises, you can habituate more quickly to the

9

surroundings. You have developed a number of pathways to eliminate the unnecessary and focus on the necessary, calm yourself, alert yourself and just do the task the needs to be done without crashing and burning. Aren't you a smarty pants? Most of your students learn the process of habituation and compensation fairly quickly. So much so that teachers aren't even aware of the environmental stimulation that these students have learned to deal with instinctively. The little guys in your class who have sensory integration dysfunction aren't any less smart, it is just harder for them to do what others can do naturally – that is, block out the irrelevant and focus on the relevant.

Ok, ok, so I am a smarty-pants, you say to yourself, but doesn't everybody have sensory dysfunction *sometimes*? I mean, you don't really want to say this out loud but, sometimes you check like twelve times to make sure the oven is off before you leave the house right? Or sometimes you want to scream "Shut Up!" when you are monitoring the lunchroom, right? Or, *some of us* feel soothed by stroking the silk on the blanket before going to sleep at night…. or not. Geez, does that mean that you have a sensory integration disorder? Relax, the answer to that one is NO. You see, everyone has sensory SENSITIVITIES that make life challenging because we are all human and stuff bugs us sometimes. The difference with children (and other people) who have Sensory Integration Dysfunction and those that don't is that these people have a great deal of difficulty functioning in daily life because of their sensory sensitivities. Their discomfort interferes significantly with their quality of life even when doing the most mundane activities such as transitioning from places and activities, sitting, moving, relating to others, eating, and personal care. In the words of Carol Stock Kranowitz, a guru and author of, "The Out of Sync Child,"

"The child with sensory integration dysfunction struggles mightily to feel in sync with the world."

Bummer.

Our job then, as teachers, is three-fold in working with children who have sensory sensitivities:

1. To manage the stimulation in the learning environment.

2. To be attuned to children's sensitivities and how this affects their behavior.

3. To create opportunities to encourage more healthy habituation.

4. To teach children ways that they can self-regulate their own sensitivities and learn to compensate.

OK, I lied the job is four-fold.

Time to Reflect

Something intrigued you to pick up this book, whether it was a student who confused you throughout the year, your own child, or even your own sensitivities to sensory stimulation. Now is your chance to identify the behavioral issues that brought this situation to your awareness. Write a paragraph about that child or student or even your own sensitivities. What kinds of behaviors are exhibited? When? What seems to set the behaviors off? When is the person most calm? How does the person react to change? What kinds of things does the person wear, eat, touch, or complain about? Write about what you have tried as strategies to deal with the behaviors. What has worked? What hasn't? What worked for a while and then stopped? What made the behavior much worse?

A Little Brainy Background

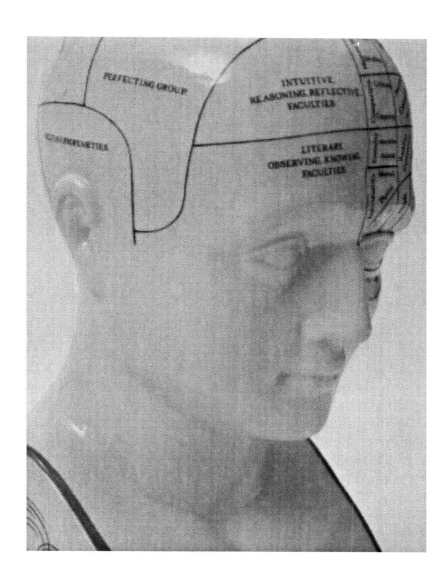

FIGHT OR FLIGHT

In primitive days, we relied on our basic instincts and senses to provide us with the necessary information to escape danger. When ancient man met a lion on the road, he would turn and run away (FLIGHT), or he would stay and defend himself against the beast, hoping for the best possible outcome (FIGHT). We were dependent on the adequate functioning of our senses and deriving meaning from them. We were then able to produce quick solutions to the dangers that threatened our very survival. Although, in our society we rarely meet the lion on the road, our brains do not distinguish between real threat and perceived threat. Real threats are those things that cause us physical harm and SHOULD instigate the survival mentality. Perceived threats are those that are not physically harmful but bring about all of the biological reactions of the survival mode

A Vignette of Modern Day Fight or Flight

Let's just say that one day, in the middle of the school year, without any warning, you are summarily called to the superintendent's office, without any indication as to the nature of the request. You do not know the superintendent personally (otherwise known as the Big Kahuna) and rarely go to the district office. Your mind immediately goes into overdrive considering the meaning of this summons. Did I do something wrong? Did I do something right? Is there something that I don't know about that I should know about? Your heart starts to beat faster and you feel warm, maybe even a little light-headed, as you ponder the ramifications of this summons. Driving over to the office, you feel dizzy and fearful, you start to perspire, and your breathing becomes quick. As you approach the superintendent's office, you notice the smells, the posters on the walls, the glare of the tiled floor and the sound of your shoes as you walk down the long empty hallway. A door slams and you are startled. The sound makes your skin feel like it has been pricked by tiny pins all over. You feel like you want to walk right out the door and pretend like you were never there. But you don't.

As you get to the door of the Big Kahuna's office, you see a secretary who looks at you sternly over her glasses and briskly asks, "May I help you?" Your voice trembles a little as you introduce yourself. She asks you to take seat in the waiting area. You do as commanded, although you would rather stand and the chair is instantly uncomfortable to you. You try not to squirm, but you cannot seem to get comfortable. You try to read a magazine on the table, but you cannot concentrate. You feel thirsty, but are reluctant to leave or ask the stern looking woman for a cup of water. It is too quiet in this office, but the ringing of a telephone intermittently interrupts the silence and the stern lady's nasal voice provides answers to questions that were posed from the other end. Your stomach churns, your mind races, your body seems foreign, and then, as you try to calm yourself, your own cell phone rings loudly in the quiet office causing you to jump so that you almost fall off of your chair. You fish out your phone from your bag, spilling everything onto the floor in the process. You realize it is your spouse needing you to pick up something at the store. Your response is less than cordial or helpful which causes their response to be less than cordial, leaving you even shakier and more confused and wanting

15

to get away and leave this office right now! Just when you think that you can't take the waiting anymore – the sounds, the sitting, the phone ringing, the nasal voice, the smells, the stale air – the stern secretary looks your way and says in a formal manner, "The SUPERINTENDENT will see you now."

In modern day, the lion in the road may take the persona of the superintendent at the district office. Although the physical threat is not the same as fighting a wild beast, our primal brains and central nervous system harkens back to those primitive times when danger was a physical threat to our survival. We respond in the same physical way as we did in the primitive days. The fight or flight response takes over in order to protect our very survival. As an adult, you have learned to use your grown-up brain to manage your fight or flight responses. Your caveman brain (apologies to all the cavemen out there) wants to run away or punch the secretary with the nasal voice in the nose. But you don't do that because your grown-up brain stops you.

When our sensory sensitive students can't switch on this other part of their brains, ANY activities that push these sensitive buttons can throw them into caveman mode. These issues can be transitioning from circle time to reading, going to the cafeteria, having someone bump them in line, or the smell of paste.

So these two parts of your brain that are working constantly in all daily experiences, are at odds with each other. There is the reasonable one, and the primal, emotional one. It is almost like the angel and the devil looking over your shoulder, but I like to think of them as the CEO and the Drama Queen.

The DRAMA QUEEN

The Drama Queen is located deep within your brain in an area called the limbic system. It is responsible for the primal emotions that cause you to react in the fight or flight response. Although we need this character to warn us of potential danger, she can be a problem when she takes over and treats even innocuous events as DANGEROUS. For the Drama Queen, emotions are always at a peak, without consideration for curbing the impulses, or political correctness (if you will) to stimuli.

THE CEO

The other part of the brain that is in direct antithesis to the limbic system is called the prefrontal cortex and is located right behind your forehead. This is the part of the brain that is your own personal CEO. It is responsible for managing your behaviors, curbing impulses, making decisions, remembering all kinds of stuff and being the ultimate multi-tasker.

For children who have sensory processing disorders, all stimuli go first to the Drama Queen rather than passing through the CEO before acting. The still developing brain misreads the environmental cues and forces all of the behaviors into a survival mode. Current research indicates that teachers in the United States today may see behavioral issues brought about by sensory dysfunction in as many as 20% of their students. Children with autism, attention deficit disorder, learning disabilities and communication disorders are more likely to have sensory issues than non-disabled children. Those children who are affected by trauma have brain changes that may be instantaneously diverted to their limbic system (Drama Queens) as their brain chemistry has been permanently altered to respond in a fight or flight mentality. The jury is still out on considering the causes for sensory disorders. Current researchers believe that a variety of conditions may be responsible, including; prenatal exposure to toxic substances, birth trauma, genetics, premature birth or early illnesses such as meningitis.

It may also be that the recent increase in the behaviors of young children with a correlation to sensory difficulties is not all biological in nature. With the fast paced, stimulating society that we live in, some of what we see in these problems with our students may actually be in response to this bustling world.

What Fight or Flight Looks Like In a Preschooler

Tantrums

Reacts excessively to touch

Screams without apparent provocation

Dislikes hugs

Refusals

NO! NO! NO!

Hyperactivity

Inability to settle into one activity

Bolting/running away

Difficulty transitioning

Failure to follow directions

Screaming

Explosive

Crying

Fussy about clothing, tags etc.

What Fight or Flight Looks Like in a School - Aged Child

Refusals

Lack of motivation

Noncompliance

Arguing

Oppositional behaviors

Mood swings

Poor social skills

Impulsivity

Inattention

Overreaction

Over or under dresses for the temperature

Hypervigilant of the environment

Complains of frequent stomach aches or headaches

Constantly making noise in a quiet environment

Crying

Explosive behavior

All behavior

is an attempt

to communicate

something.

WHAT AM I COMMUNICATING THAT I NEED?

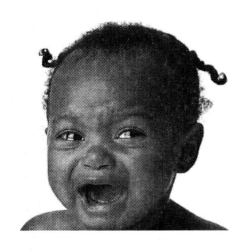

Avoidance

Escape

Stimulation

Attention

Desire

Power

Physical/Organic

Revenge

Intensity, Duration and Frequency

Most misbehaviors demonstrated by children can really be considered "minor" in nature. What turns a minor misbehavior into something that is problematic and therefore challenging to adults, are three elements: the *intensity* with which the behavior is displayed; the *duration* in which the behavior occurs; and, the *frequency* of it happening. Let's look at a behavior that would typically occur in the classroom and examine it in light of these three characteristics.

Raheim and Jaleshia are both "challenging" children.

Scenario One

While lining up to go to lunch, Jaleshia becomes very upset when her classmate accidentally bumps into her. She screams as though the other child beat her unmercifully (*intensity*). This happens every day (*frequency)* as the students line up to go somewhere. It stops the class from functioning for that period of time that it takes to calm Jaleshia down. It takes some time, (*duration*) but she finally calms and the offending classmate issues a puzzled apology, so the line starts to move down the hallway to the lunchroom. While walking to the cafeteria, Jaleshia walks far behind the rest of the class forcing you, the teacher, to continually call her name and ask her to hurry up. At this suggestion, she holds her hands over her ears and yells, "I'm COMING!" in a not-so-respectful tone. You leave the front of the line to retrieve her, and she refuses to hold your hand. At this point she bolts from the line and pushes her way to the lunchroom door pushing the other children who are calmly waiting their turns out of the way. She loudly states at this time, "I hate this place, it smells like barf!" (*intensity*). Such is the scene every day (*frequency*) during the class to lunchroom transition (*duration*). Get the idea?

Scenario Two

This morning, Raheim woke up on the wrong side of the bed. When lining up to go to the cafeteria, he pushed his way to the front of the line even though he knew he wasn't the line leader. When told to go to the back of the line, he did so with a smirk on his face and then started pestering those who were in front of him by making bathroom noises. When told to quiet down, he did so, but not before he made one last raspberry sound on his arm and accidentally spit on the little girl in front of him. When you give him the "teacher eye" and reprimand him, he apologizes to the girl, quiets down and you don't have any further issues with him.

The difference between Rahiem and Jaleshia is not the kind of behaviors they exhibit; both had difficulty following the rules to line up and walk peacefully to the cafeteria. In these two scenarios, what differs is the **intensity** with which the behavior occurs. In Jaleshia's case she upsets the entire class by being very vocal, and is not able to be managed by typical discipline techniques. Her behavior also differs in the **frequency** that these outbursts occur (it happens every day, and every time the class lines up for lunch). Rahiem, on the other hand, has a bad day *once in a while*. The **duration** of the two behaviors is considerably different as well. Jaleshia's behavior escalates throughout the transition time and does not calm with minor interventions. Her outbursts escalate and last longer because she is unable to calm at an earlier point. Because Rahiem responds to minor interventions, he calms down, and thus the duration of his problematic behavior is lessened.

While both children demonstrated "oppositional" behaviors, one was challenging and problematic due to intensity, duration and frequency. The same "behavior" with the other child can be considered *minor* due to the LACK of intensity, duration and frequency. For children with sensory integration difficulties, who are always attempting to stimulate themselves, reduce the stimulation or integrate the sensory experiences around them, their responses WILL differ in intensity, duration and frequency than their peers.

It Just Makes Sense(s)!

Your SEVEN Senses

When we think of the senses that help us to interact with the world, most of us think of sight, hearing, touch, taste and smell. In the vernacular of sensory integration disorders, these are considered "far senses." These senses require that you take information in from afar (or from the environment) in order to translate it into meaning in your brain. When there is an inefficiency or ineffectiveness with one or more of these senses, the world becomes a confusing place and routine tasks become daunting. Remember the childhood game of being blindfolded and having someone lead you through a maze? The unfamiliarity of those objects and movements that were previously comfortable or non-existent, now have become threatening in the perceived danger they may pose. You were temporarily without the "far sense" of sight.

What is equally important in the realm of processing sensory information into meaning is the role of two other senses, which are considered "near senses." Near senses are those that are internal to the individual and it is only when faced with a task that requires facilitating them that it becomes apparent the extent of the impact and the deficit. One near sense is defined as *vestibular*, which has to do with balance, gravity, and the ability to move with stability. The other near sense is *proprioceptive*, which is the ability to translate sensory information through our muscles and joints. All seven senses are necessary to consider when planning helpful interventions for children with sensory integration deficits. In this section you will:

1. Become familiar with sensory integration and dysfunction issues relating to each sense.
2. Do an empathy activity to help you truly understand from an emotional standpoint what it feels like to have one of these difficulties.
3. Be provided with a whole bunch of adaptations that you can easily apply to the environment, your teaching, the routine, or to the student assignments

AND you will get TONS of ideas for creating lessons or learning centers for helping these children learn sensory integration concepts, otherwise known as creating a balanced "sensory diet". (Well maybe not *tons. . .*)

Auditory

Imagine ......

If the humming of the lights were louder than your teacher's voice.

When someone whispers it feels like they are yelling.

When someone moves his or her chair on the floor it feels like sharp pricks all over your skin.

The only time that you can really concentrate is when you are humming or talking.

Too many noises in a confined space make you feel nauseated.

You have to wear a hat or a hood all of the time, just to block other noises.

You cannot concentrate in a quiet place AT ALL.

You cannot concentrate in a noisy place AT ALL.

You cannot walk when there is background noise.

A fire alarm goes off and you feel pain as though you have been shot.

Characteristics

Auditory input is what we hear and what is transmitted to the brain to make meaning of sounds. Children who suffer from sensory sensitivities in auditory perception will have a very difficult time in a traditional classroom setting due to the varying and constantly distracting levels of noise that active learning produces. Learning in an elementary classroom requires a certain level of interaction and happy, busy chatter to be effective. The child who has sensory processing problems in the auditory area may:

Have "selective" hearing

Appear deaf

Put his hands over his ears

Become very upset by loud noises

Be unable to hear where sound is coming from

Have trouble putting thoughts into spoken or written words

Have trouble responding to other people's questions and comments

Have trouble correcting or revising what she has said so as to be understood

Have a weak vocabulary and use immature sentence grammar and syntax

Have difficulty reading aloud

Improve his or her speaking ability after intensive movement

Be distractible

Be inattentive

Be distressed by noises

Watch other people before acting

Be the last one to follow directions

Become very upset transitioning to other environments (noisier or quieter)

Talk too loudly

Bang on things, make sound effects, hum, talk incessantly, talk to self

Complain that others are screaming at him

Hear noises that others do not hear

Startle in response to noises that may not be heard by others

Environmental Adaptations

Here are some ideas to try...

Provide a quiet area to escape from auditory distractions.

Seat the child in a less distracting area.

Consider using an FM system available through your district special education department.

Have a set of headphones and earplugs available.

Consider using a Yaker Tracker (a device to monitor classroom noise with a visual cue).

Allow older children to use an iPod® to listen to music (dispensed by you).

Seat them by a white noise machine or fish tank.

Put tennis balls on chair legs to cut down on noise from chairs on hard surfaces.

Allow the child to wear his hood or hat to block out stimuli.

Be an active listener.

Simplify your language.

Allow for adequate processing time.

Reward behavior with nonverbal gestures such as smiles, hugs and high fives

Stimulate language development by talking about things while the children are working.

Use mnemonic devices to help with memory.

Get the child's attention before giving directions.

Have a cue that allows the child to know that he or she will be the next to answer a question.

Do not require reading aloud.

Give brief, concise directions.

Be aware that these children may not appropriately process the tone, cadence and nuances of language. Volume can be misinterpreted.

Experiment with different types of music in the classroom to see what calms and what arouses this child.

Warn the child prior to noisy intrusions (yes, even a fire drill).

Consider using sound reducing materials in the classroom (e.g., carpeting rather than hard surfaces).

Activities

To integrate, stimulate or calm the AUDITORY SENSE

Use a slide whistle to create movement patterns for the children to respond to.

Make or purchase different percussion or rhythmic instruments such as shakers, lummi sticks, drums, etc. for lessons in sound location.

Make paper plate tambourines for tapping out rhythms.

Have the children guess songs by tapping out rhythms.

Play a game matching sounds using two film canisters that contain the same objects.

Use hula-hoops set up on the floor (one per child) to move from one to another with music (this is a good lesson for teaching individual space lessons as well).

Do rhyming activities.

Play "Mother May I" or "Simon Says."

Make paintings using straws or blow pens to make the consonant sounds, B G K T P.

Do animal movements to their sounds (available on recordings through teacher supply catalogs).

Make picture cards for matching sounds to their environment (home sounds such as water dripping, lawn mowers or school sounds such as pencil sharpener, stapler, etc.).

Have children draw to music from classical to jazz to hip-hop to movie theme songs (this is better with instrumental music, however).

Make a rubber band harp by taking a sturdy cigar box (or something that size) and stretching rubber bands over the narrow ends over the box.

Play tunes or sing and march in place with the rubber band harp.

Make and play a tune on a water glass xylophone, eight drinking glasses with varying levels of water in them so create musical melodies.

How it feels

This is an activity that may give you a sense of what it is like to have auditory processing deficit.

In a group, number-off from one to ten. Each person is the bird that corresponds with his or her number. Get up and move around the room, make only your bird sound and see if you can find your mate simply by "calling" to them.

Bird	Sound it makes
1.Ovenbird	Teacher teacher teacher
2. Northern cardinal	What cheer cheer cheer
3. Eastern towhee	Drink your tree
4. White Throated sparrow	Please please Canada Canda Canada
5. Tutfed titmouse	Peter peter peter
6. Black capped chicadee	Chicka dee dee dee
7. Cactus Wren	Cha-cha-cha-cha-cha
8. Red winged blackbird	Konk a ree
9. California Quail	Chi-ca-go
10. Dove	Who cooks for you?

After participating in this exercise, what would have helped you to feel more comfortable? Write down a few ideas for adaptations of your own.

_____

_____

visual

Imagine if. . .

The bright sunlight made you sick to your stomach but you had to do all of your work outside on sunny days.

You couldn't focus your eyes on one thing because everything else catches your attention and your eyes landed there instead.

The only color you could tolerate was gray and you hated other colors because they made you feel sick.

Even dim lights were so bright that you had to squint, and then you get a pounding headache from the squinting.

You couldn't write down notes or copy information because you keep losing your place.

It was very uncomfortable to look someone in the eye.

You could not perceive depth, location, distance and space between objects such that a task like driving felt like an optical illusion.

You literally could not "see the forest for the trees."

You couldn't catch a ball because you are so intent on watching your arms that you didn't watch the ball.

Characteristics

Visual input is what we see and what is transmitted to the brain to make meaning of visual stimuli. Children who suffer from sensory sensitivities in visual perception will have a very difficult time in a primary classroom setting due to the intensity of the visual stimuli (bright posters, children's art work, alphabet strips and number lines, birthday cutouts, calendar and weather charts, etc.). And, when we run out of wall space, things hang things from the ceiling so they can twist every time there is the slightest hint of a breeze. Goodness! If that is not enough, visuals are also used with heavy reliance to teach new concepts in elementary classrooms.

The child who has sensory processing problems in the visual area may. . .

Prefer to be in the dark

Hesitate in going up and down steps

Avoid bright lights

Stare intensely at people or objects

Avoid eye contact

Shield his eyes to screen out sights

Close or cover one eye or squint, complaining of seeing double

Tilt his head when reading across the page

Tilt her body when watching TV or the teacher at circle time

Have difficulty tracking or following a moving object

Be unable to follow a line of print

Confuse similarities and differences in pictures and words

Omit words or numbers or loses his place frequently when reading

Have difficulty with fine motor tasks

Constantly bump into objects in the environment; be uncomfortable with moving objects or people

Confuse right and left and often turn the wrong way

Not understand concepts of up/down, before/after and first/second

Fail to visualize what is read

Withdraw from group activities where movement is required

Environmental Adaptations

Here are some ideas to try…

Consider a "growing classroom": keep the visual distractions to a minimum at the beginning of the year and gradually add new things.

Use fabric and Velcro® to hide clutter on bookshelves.

Use solid colored fabrics in muted colors instead of patterned ones.

Use preferential seating to eliminate distractions (front of the classroom, away from a busy activity spot).

Seat the student away from the window to avoid the distraction of outdoors and changing light conditions.

Create a space that is visually distraction-free in the room so that he/she can escape to it.

Experiment with different lighting sources; natural, lamps, full spectrum lights.

Do not require copying from the board; give the child his or her own copy of what is being copied by others.

Have a study-buddy for this child, for taking notes from the board on duplicate paper.

Be highly organized.

Remove excess visual displays.

Create visual boundaries.

Utilize rudimentary picture schedules and individualize them.

Have a consistent notebook system for papers that are to be turned in and those that are to be completed (page 107).

Provide colored report-cover overlays to tone down visual glare.

Provide lined paper for assignments

Place the child's desk where is faces a non-visually distracting area.

Use opaque containers with labels in subtle colors for organization.

Be aware of those colors that stimulate the central nervous system (bright yellows, reds and oranges) and those that calm (blues and greens).

Use colors in the classroom judiciously.

Create visual boundaries for desks, playground areas, and personal space.

Use cones for outdoor areas, brightly colored "painters tape" for desks, and carpet squares for circle time.

Allow the child to wear a ball cap or visor to block out overhead light.

Use graph paper and special writing paper with highlighted lines for written work (page 104).

Allow for additional processing time for visual, motor and transitioning tasks.

Allow for visual breaks by instructing the children to close their eyes and lead them through a guided relaxation activity.

Surround the child with others who sit quietly and pay attention.

Prepare worksheets that have lots of white space around the problems.

Seat the child near the teacher, away from the distracting movements of other children.

DO NOT hang things from the ceiling so that they flutter in the breeze.

Adjust Venetian blinds to prevent sunshine from flickering through.

Activities

To integrate, stimulate or calm the VISUAL SENSE

Teach students to use configuration cues for words (page 105).

Develop learning centers that require ordering the sizes of objects.

Play games with paddleballs.

Have children organize the schedule board.

Have children identify objects in a paper bag by touch.

Practice having children roll a ball with partners, between their legs while seated in a v-position on the ground.

Have the child roll a ball between his legs into a paper sack while seated in a v-position.

Play a game of catch with a Velcro® mitt.

Peel and eat fruit, section it.

Peel and eat dried fruit sheet rolls.

Make non-competitive games out of beanbag tosses.

For a math activity, make gutter out of vinyl house gutters and have students race different objects to determine speed and distance.

Create bar graphs of numbers of activities, preferences or objects around the room.

Utilize lessons that require "guess- tamation" of the number of objects.

Water plants with a spouted water pail.

Be the fish tank helper: have the student clean, feed and scoop up fish.

Play "Simon Says."

Identify patterns throughout the day.

Use flashlights to track a moving light.

Use a flashlight to have the child jump from spot to spot or focus on one object.

Fill the sand tray with buried small figurines.

Encourage sand play with various sifting toys.

Develop a textile-learning center for making fabric items, sewing or experimentation with textures.

Have the child organize and nestle stacking boxes.

Reinstitute the age-old "fishing game" using a pole with a magnet on the end of the line to pick up "fish."

Play catch with cut out plastic milk cartons as scoops and a soft ball.

Have the children order a number of small items and develop a bar graph to show comparisons.

Identify facial expressions utilizing a "How do you feel?" chart (available in counseling and teacher supply catalogs).

Create lessons that minimize verbal interaction and allow the child to rely on visual or motor explanations.

Have children develop and utilize word or sentence windows (page 106).

Teach keyboarding.

Have them fold papers in half so that only 50% of the printed material is showing.

Have the child highlight the directions on each handout.

Use verbal reminders for transitions.

Create lessons in which older children can use a video recorder to make "commercials" about a concept.

Do not require copying from the board.

Have the child color in all of the Os in a newspaper or other printed material as a calming activity.

Teach students to juggle scarves and set up a juggling area in the class utilizing a three-minute hourglass or egg timer to indicate the length of the break time.

How it Feels

De   wn staris to poi h
   tsywe   ntdo   erprotherTomfro   m
Break   t. The   tapl saw   setwit
    Fast   hcubs
ora   nd bowls
   ngejuicea   of ce   realth athr athe rpad   hab setout
th   atmorn   ingbe   fore   e leftgorwork   angeju
       d ce   real a
an,   gaintho   ughtBe   tsy   Why sieve rthyi
                                                              ng

al   s the
     way   sa   me a   roundhere   ?   He   rthou
                                                                         ghts

where in   rupted   Tomwho ie   out
       ter   dy   t

aloud   , wipe   his mou   th   with sih sle
      bitch   d

ve   anp   sladded he   ron   the   ad, his way of sayin
                                            he   g
se   let   er
eye

Betsy went downstairs to join her brother Tom for breakfast. The table was set with
cups, orange juice and bowls of cereal that her father had set out that morning before he
left for work. Orange juice and cereal again, thought Betsy. Why is everything always
the same around here? Her thoughts were interrupted by Tom who let out a loud belch,
wiped his mouth with his sleeve and slapped her on the head, his way of saying, see ya
later.

Smell

Did you know that the olfactory sense is the one far sensation that has a direct connection

to the limbic system of the brain? Smell doesn't have to detour to other areas for memory or meaning, smell just leaps directly to the part of the brain that is responsible for emotions. This is the reason why you may smell something and it will immediately trigger a memory from long ago. Just as the wonderful smells of cinnamon, lavender and gingerbread may bring you instantly back to visits to grandmother's house and make you feel warm, nurtured and calm, so can unpleasant smells bring back difficult memories that can set off behaviors in children because the smell has been perceived as threatening. Guess what? Life stinks

sometimes. We will need to help this child to discriminate between gross smells and nice smells.

Characteristics

The olfactory sense is what we smell and what is transmitted to the brain to make meaning of smelly stimuli. It is a bit2005 this sensory integration problem, because what may be escalating this child's behavior is not always evident to other people. Children who suffer from sensory sensitivities in smell will intermittently have behavioral difficulties (unprovoked, so it seems). They will tell you that you stink, and will plug their little cherub noses often. They may react in an extreme manner when entering the cafeteria, or when the cooking smells waft down the hallway to your classroom. All of these stimuli are unbeknownst to you and the others because you have learned to HABITUATE (remember that word?), or, you don't consider these smells to be gross, stinky, barfy or disgusting.

Children with olfactory dysfunction may:

> Smell everything/one before interacting with it/them
>
> Smell odors and/or be strongly affected by odors that others do not notice
>
> Strongly object to odors that seem subtle to others
>
> Be a picky eater
>
> Be under sensitive to smells that others find objectionable
>
> Be unaware of personal hygiene and not take measures to correct it
>
> Have extreme behavioral reactions to odors
>
> Plug their noses frequently
>
> State that things smell bad often
>
> Desire strongly spiced foods or very bland foods
>
> Dislike certain people because of their smell
>
> Sniff people or objects
>
> Not notice offensive smells

Environmental Adaptations

Here are some ideas to try...

Use aromatherapy to help drown out smells or to relax and calm.

Experiment with different scents; what might be relaxing for some may be stimulating to others.

Explore scents with the child to find the ones that work best to meet the goal to either stimulate or soothe.

Peppermint and citrus can be stimulating and help arouse the senses and alertness.

Lavender and vanilla are generally soothing and help to calm the senses.

Have the student carry a bottle of the smell when intolerance hits.

Be aware of the smells that are in your classroom during certain art activities, science, parties, meal preparation or if you have animals in your classroom.

Allow the child opportunities to escape the smell – run an errand, go outside, etc.

Consider using odor eliminators in your classroom.

Seat the child away from such olfactory distractions as the cafeteria or the gerbil cage.

Keep animals, paint supplies and other aromatic materials away from the child's desk.

Activities

To develop healthy integration of the OLFACTORY SENSE

Introduce activities slowly and with caution

- Play "Smello" (like bingo, with film canisters).
- Play "Smash and Smell"- have a collection of different scents, a rubber mallet a tally sheet at a learning center to allow the children to pound the scents and experiment with them, graphing the smells in order of good to yucky.
- Fill pill bottles or film canisters with scented cotton balls, have students categorize the scents – good, bad, clean, dirty, spicy, etc.
- Have students make scented flash cards with scented glue, markers and stickers.
- Water down glue and use glue sticks rather than paste.
- Talk to the child about his or her own odors if they have under-sensitivity to personal hygiene issues and develop personal hygiene lessons for the class.

Consider aromatherapy! Typically, these are calming and arousing scents:

Calming	Arousing Scents
gingerbread	chocolate
vanilla extract	coffee
sugar cookie	dirt
chamomile	lemon or orange
apples	pencil shavings
banana	mothballs
butter	onions /garlic
crayons	oregano
baby powder	rubber
pine needles	mint

Have students make their own potpourri with supplies of dried mint, spices, cloves, nutmeg, cinnamon, flower petals: rose, lilac, and lavender. Put everything in a baby food jar and shake it. Voila! Potpourri

TASTE

Characteristics

The input of information through our taste buds is how we first learn to experience the world around us. When things are working right, this input is transmitted to the brain to make meaning of food. Children who suffer from sensory sensitivities in taste perception will become more difficult when it comes to snack or lunchtime (for obvious reasons). But they may also have a problem with eating or tasting *everything* (paint, glue, paste, pencil shavings, erasers) so that they can stimulate their senses to make meaning of it. This can be a bit of a problem for safety reasons, huh? Children, who have sensory processing difficulties in the far sense of taste, may exhibit the following characteristics:

> Be VERY PICKY eaters
>
> Claim that all food tastes the same
>
> Will only eat very bland foods
>
> Become agitated or fearful of the cafeteria
>
> Will not join in with treats
>
> Will not eat at school
>
> Refuse to eat at all
>
> Require excessive amounts of salt, pepper and spices
>
> Won't eat certain textures of food
>
> Only eat certain textures of food
>
> Unwilling to try new foods
>
> Chew on everything
>
> Eat non-edibles*

Since the sense of gustatory sense is so closely tied with the olfactory sense, many of the same characteristics for the child with smell sensitivities will be true for the child who has taste sensitivities. More attention, however, is paid to the texture and temperatures of foods with the difficulties in processing taste.

*A word of caution! If you have a student who INGESTS non-edibles (doesn't just TASTE them) it may be a sign of a more serious problem and will need referral to your counselor or school psychologist.

Environmental Adaptations

Here are some ideas to try...

Do not force new foods without preparation and introduction.

Have a variety of foods at each mealtime.

Make mealtime peaceful.

Plant a garden and taste the creations.

Use a straw to suck up denser foods (yogurt and applesauce).

Allow for drinking water from a bottle at the student's desk.

Allow for chewing on a straw, coffee stir stick or rubber tubing at the end of a pencil.

Use the "lick" rather than "take-a-bite-rule".

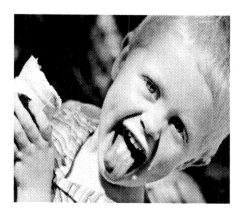

Activities

To develop healthy integration of the sense of TASTE

Encourage the student to take a *lick* instead of a *bite* of new foods.

Teach the students to cook.

Have the children help with making snacks.

Choose a theme for food activities and centers: citrus, round, colorful, long or stringy.

Play Taste-O! like Bing-O! with tastes.

Tactile

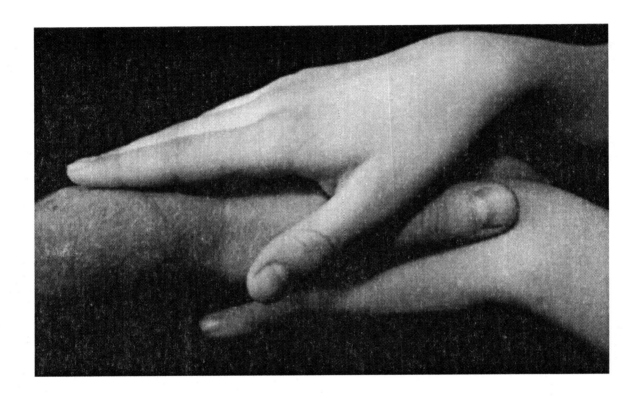

Some thirty inches from my nose
The frontier of my person goes
And all the untilled air between
Is private pagus or demise.
Stranger, unless with bedroom eyes
I beckon you to fraternize
Beware of rudely crossing it
I have no gun but I can spit.

W.H. Auden
Prologue: *"The Birth of Adventure"*

We are all aware of our own personal space, the two to four feet that surrounds you and is the protective bubble between you and the rest of the world. Research indicates that "social space" is typically four to eight feet in work and social gatherings. "Public space" distance is said to be nine to ten feet. Of course these dimensions differ according to the culture. In eastern cultures, for instance, the distance is considerably smaller, while in native cultures the distance can be considerably greater. Tactile input is what we feel and what is transmitted to the brain to make meaning of touch. Children who suffer from tactile sensitivities will be challenging no matter how you approach it. There is so much touch going on in an elementary classroom, that it can be considered a primary form of communication. There is tactile input from your peers, from the teacher, to your teacher, while investigating new experiences, every time a new art project is introduced, when lining up to go somewhere, even when the weather changes! We can't get away from tactile stimulus. For children with sensory integration difficulties in the tactile sense, life is a constant barrage of challenges at school.

Characteristics

The child who has tactile integration issues may show the following characteristics:

Touches everyone, but reacts excessively when someone touches them

Responds negatively to light touch

Likes roughhouse play

Dislikes surprises

Lacks in understanding of different sensations (e.g., a raindrop might feel the same as a thorn)

Not learn from painful mistakes (repeatedly touches the hot stove)

Strongly resists being touched by teacher, nurse, barber

Becomes distracted and fidgety during quiet concentration times

Becomes upset with changes in weather and wind or with insects

Fusses about clothing, especially new or stiff clothing

Avoids touching certain textures

Avoids touch sensation activities (finger painting, food, textiles)

Is very sensitive to air and object temperatures

Lacks or has a heightened awareness of body temperature

Over dresses or under dresses for the weather

Is excessively bothered by the seams in clothing

Wants all tags in clothing removed

Refuses to wear a belt or anything that ties around the waist or neck

Prefers cotton

Dislikes brushing teeth, hair brushing and avoids personal care activities

Aversion to going barefoot or having feet touched

Arms himself at all times with a stick or toy or hand-held weapon

Stands still against traffic in a group

Rationalizes to avoid touch sensations, "My mom told me not to get my hands dirty."

Seems unaware of touch unless it is very intense

Shows little reaction to pain or keeps making painful mistakes over and over

Is a messy dresser

Unable to identify body parts without touching them

Seems out-of-touch with his hands

Difficulty holding scissors, crayons and forks

Seems compelled to touch certain surfaces that cause others discomfort

Seeks messy experiences

Rubs own skin excessively

Difficulty perceiving physical properties of objects: temperature, size, weight

Unable to identify objects just by touch

Vocabulary is limited due to inexperience with tactile sensations

Exhibits poor self-help skills

Withdraws from physical, art, music or science activities

Acts silly

Has poor peer relations or is a loner

Is stubborn, inflexible and rigid

Environmental Adaptations

Here are some ideas to try...

Allow the child to wear his or her outerwear in the classroom.

Warn the child before touching.

Seat the child at the head of the table or at the edge of the rug to lessen contact with others.

Approach the child from the front before touching.

Give the child a visual cue that touch is coming.

Use firm pressure on the shoulder or back rather than to brush a sleeve or arm.

Put the child's desk at the periphery of the room out of traffic so that others don't bump into him.

Allow the small child to sit on the adults lap during circle time.

Use mechanical pencils if the child uses too much pressure when writing.

Provide pencil grips for proper alignment of the grasp.

Allow the child to wear a favorite sweatshirt rather than insist it be hung up with the others.

Allow child to use paintbrushes or tongue depressors instead of finger painting.

Put paints and a little bit of hair gel (a little dab will do ya) in a Ziploc® baggie, allow the child to do "non-messy finger-painting" this way.

Use play dough or silly putty as a pencil grip!

Activities

To develop healthy integration of the TACTILE SENSE

- Teach the children how to care for class pet with gentle touch.
- Develop personal space lessons; hula-hoops work well or drawing an outline of the child's body on butcher paper. Talk about the "bubble" of everyone's space that exists outside of the body. Instruct children not to invade someone else's space unless they have been invited.
- Use shaving cream as an "unpaint"; squirt it on a cookie sheet and smoosh it around, write letters, draw shapes etc. Drive cars through the shaving cream, making shapes and tracks with it
- Have a variety of textures available for "fiddling": oobleck, play dough, Space Dough®, etc.
- Make oobleck from equal parts cornstarch and water.
- Have the children make custard, pudding or Jell-O Jigglers.
- Use cold cooked spaghetti in a learning center to manipulate into shapes, letters or numbers and let them dry on a cookie sheet or cardboard before they are painted.
- When you make play dough, make it plain at first. A few days later add color and have the children help to work it through the dough. A few days after that have the children add in scents and work it in – very individualized play dough! Make sure to dust the children's fingers with flour so the play dough doesn't stick too much to their fingers.
- Hide little toys in a sand tray or play dough. Hunt for the little toys and then have the children sort them into egg carton containers.

- Play "Simon Says."
- Create a "tactile road" using different textures, carpet squares, sandpaper, Astroturf, satin, bubble wrap, foam egg-crate bedding, and pillow cases filled with rice, beans, or large beads and have the children walk barefoot across it.
- Make handprints out of plaster or paint.

- Have the children wrap each other up in "mummy wraps" using a large roll of crepe paper (children need to be standing for this exercise).

- Make a child "hot dog" by having the child lay floor on a blanket and wrap him up like a hot dog. Roll him back and forth and then "add" condiments, by pantomime, brushing on mustard and ketchup and piling on the onions! Using this kind of activity prior to a sensory sensitive experience can lessen the defensiveness for most children.

- Have a tactile learning center that has all things from nature to examine, touch and manipulate. Provide tweezers, film canisters, magnifying glasses, tape, trays and small dishes, small spoons as tools for investigation.

- For an outdoor activity provide each child with a hula-hoop that they plop down somewhere so they can analyze that area within their "ecosystem".

- Use tweezers and small containers to collect elements of the ecosystem. Take notes, graph and chart the elements, and dump everything back onto the ecosystem when done.

- Another outdoor activity is to make a bracelet of masking tape with the sticky side out. Have the children collect things from outdoors that make a unique bracelet – little flowers, pebbles, feathers, grasses, etc.

Make your own play dough:
>   2 cups of flour
>   1 cup of salt
>   4 teaspoons of cream of tartar
>   2 cups of water
>   4 tablespoons of vegetable oil

In a large pot stir the flour, salt, cream of tartar, water and oil over very low heat until the dough comes away from the edge of the pot and makes a soft ball, let the play dough cool. Store in an airtight container.

Make your own oobleck:
Mix equal parts water and cornstarch together in a large bowl. This substance will form a consistency that is a liquid when not being handled, a solid when being handled.

Motion, Movement and Balance
(Vestibular)

Imagine if you had to do everything in a shaky rowboat- stand, jump, walk, read, listen your students, talk on the phone, make dinner, drive a car.

Characteristics

The vestibular sense is what we feel by movement and what is transmitted to the brain to make meaning of gravity, balance and movement. Children who suffer from sensory sensitivities in the vestibular sense have difficulty moving, sitting, walking, climbing and standing. If you have ever had a vertigo-induced experience brought on by your spouse's great fascination with deep-sea fishing, a ride on Space Mountain, or an inner ear infection, you have a little bit of an understanding of what this child feels in the area of a vestibular processing disorder. Children who have problems with the near sense of vestibular integration or are over or under stimulated by this sense may demonstrate the following characteristics:

Have poor balance

Have difficulty going up and down stairs

Are accident-prone

Bump into things often

Have a fear of elevators or escalators

Deliberately crash into people or things

Jump on furniture after repeatedly being told not to

Love rough housing

Hate rough housing

Fall out of their chairs unpredictably

Break toys inadvertently

Can't stand in line without touching other people or bumping into them

Hug too hard

Poke holes in their paper while writing or erasing

Put things down with a crash

Are fearful of the playground

Love to spin

Hate to spin

Seem to be unwilling, uncooperative or a "sissy"

Fearful of falling where no real threat exists

Fearful when someone moves him or slides his chair closer to the table

Are cautious, slow moving and hesitant in taking risks

Demand physical support from an adult

Need to keep moving, wiggles in chair, has trouble staying still

Vigorous head shaking

Rocking or jumping up and down

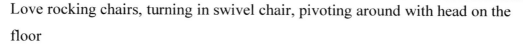

Love rocking chairs, turning in swivel chair, pivoting around with head on the floor

A thrill seeker on the playground

Doesn't get dizzy, even after spinning for long periods of time

Loves to swing

Refuses to do movement activities with music

Sits on the floor in a "W" position

Slumps or sprawls in his chair or would rather lie down than sit

Appears uncoordinated and clumsy

Can't keep a rhythmical beat

Doesn't display a hand preference by age 4 or 5

Doesn't cross the midline during fine motor activities such as painting

Unorganized or has a hard time getting organized

Difficulty with "Simon Says" and other motor planning activities

Environmental Adaptations

Here are some ideas to try...

Consider alternative forms of seating such as a stability ball, cushion, t-stool, or partially inflated stadium seat or molded child-sized plastic lawn chairs.

Use tension straps on the legs of chairs for the student to press against.

Use yoga straps for tension bands.

Allow time to use a rocking chair as "time in" (see page 90).

Provide ample warning for transitions.

Warn the child before touching him.

Use music to signal the transition to a new activity.

Help the child to "organize the sensory input" by teaching strategies such as deep breathing, placing his hands on his head, "hold up the walls", or "push down the walls."

Allow for fiddling with small objects.

Take safe movement breaks to stand up and stretch between classroom activities.

Allow children to have "crunch snack" breaks (pretzels, carrot sticks, etc.).

Allow the child to stand rather than sit at the desk or even work on the floor (tummy time).

Performance improves in writing activities when chewing gum or sucking on hard candy.

Provide opportunities for movement that are in the form of teacher errands.

Provide vertical surface for writing to help build strength in wrists and shoulders.

Have the child use an easel or desk easel.

Remind the student to use his non-dominant hand to stabilize his paper.

Give step-by-step directions for motor planning assistance.

Adjust the chair and table to the correct height (feet touching floor, elbows comfortable on the surface).

Have the child be the first to come to circle time so that he doesn't have to walk around others to find a place.

Have him sit at the end of the table during snack or group activities and offer him a chair with arms.

Have the child hold hands with an adult or peer during movement activities.

Activities

To develop healthy integration of the VESTIBULAR SENSE

Have the student

Staple papers onto bulletin boards.

Sharpen pencils with a manual sharpener.

Help the custodian by emptying waster baskets.

Put chairs on top of the desks at the end of the day.

Carry reams of paper from office to class.

Carry a box of books from one location to another.

Use the cutout machine for making letters for bulletin boards.

Help the gym teacher move mats.

Erase the chalkboard.

Fill crates to take materials from one room to another for activities.

Shovel snow, rake leaves.

Push a cart of books in the library.

Cut out items from oak tag paper.

Carry his backpack from place to place with the appropriate weight.

Push the lunch or milk cart.

Be the door monitor and hold it open for others.

Use a toy truck filled with blocks to knock down other blocks.

This student needs:

Ample time on the playground equipment.

Activity in running and jumping sports.

To do animal walks, crab crawl, bear walk.

To do scooter board activities.

Opportunities to use a mini-trampoline and jump to a beat.

To play cars on all four, pushing the toy so the child has to creep and crawl.

To have the opportunity to do his homework lying on his stomach propped up on his elbows (tummy time).

To push against a wall for stress relief.

Swing on a trapeze.

To do chair exercises, or isometrics.

How it feels

On the following page you will find a series of exercises. Complete these exercises in the time allotted.

You may NOT
Touch either arm to the table
Touch the chair with your back
Talk to others

YOU MUST
Close one eye
Lift one foot off of the floor six inches
Use your non-dominant hand to write with

After participating in this exercise, what would have helped you to feel more comfortable? Write down a few ideas for adaptations of your own.

_____

_____

_____

_____

Make the designs below with your quickest and neatest ability

Trace this design as you recite the alphabet backwards

Write the address of your school quickly in cursive without lifting your pencil while humming "Yankee Doodle".

Joints and Muscles
(Proprioceptive)

The near sense of proprioception is what we feel in our joints and muscles, which is then transmitted to the brain to make meaning of stimuli to help us plan motor movements efficiently and effectively. It is the unconscious sense of body movement. Do you remember learning a new sport such a water skiing or tennis? Have you taken a dance class and learned a new step, (I mean since junior high school)? Have you tried to thread a needle with your non-dominant hand using only a hand mirror to guide you? I didn't think so. Because if you had to do that sort of thing all the time and in a certain time frame you MIGHT get a LITTLE TASTE of what children who suffer from sensory dysfunction in the area of proprioception must feel. Because these activities are difficult for us, we choose to avoid them. Children who have difficulty in the area of proprioception cannot avoid the everyday activities of moving, sitting, writing and personal care. So guess, what? These children demonstrate "difficult behaviors" to try to escape or avoid this constant strain and stress.

61

Characteristics

The child who has difficulty in this sense may:

Demonstrate a poor sense of body awareness or where his body is in space; where his body ends and another person's body begins

Be clumsy or seem not to know how to move his body

Have difficulty pumping herself on the swings

Have trouble learning new gross motor tasks

Be hesitant to climb on play equipment

Be overly cautious about new places and activities involving movement

Have difficulty with hopping, jumping and running as age appropriate

Have difficulty with simple self-care tasks such as buttoning a shirt

Spill his food and have food all over his clothes and face

Have poor manners at the table

Be unable to control or monitor his gross or fine motor movements

Tackle everything and everybody

Show confusion walking down the street, on the playground, moving from class to class

Have difficulty crossing the midline

Write or draw with one hand and switch hands when crossing to the other side of the paper

Have a poor grip on heavy objects or lightweight objects inappropriate for the task

Be fearful when moving in space

Fall out of his chair regularly

Have difficulty climbing stairs or catching a ball

Like to be tightly swaddled

Prefer tight belts and shoelaces and hoods to help him decipher where his body is in relation to the clothing

Chew constantly on objects

Not be able to position his body when someone is helping him on with his coat or shoes

Break pencil lead easily when writing

Pick up objects with more force than necessary causing spills or breakage

Be unable to lift heavy objects because he doesn't use enough force

Slump in his chair or sit awkwardly

Always keeps one foot on the floor for stability

Not be able to keep his balance while standing on one foot

Environmental Adaptations

Here are some ideas to try...

Give simple step-by-step directions.

Use a consistent approach when teaching new skills.

Use a timer for transitions.

Warn about transitions.

Use a picture schedule.

Allow for extra time with written work.

Consider other alternatives to handwriting such as dictation or keyboarding.

Decrease the amount of written work required.

Create an obstacle course increasing in complexity throughout several days.

Play "Simon Says" or other sequencing games.

Let the child come first to circle time so he doesn't have to plan around moving between others.

Use carpet squares or another form of visual that indicates personal space boundaries.

Adjust the chair and table height to the student (the elbow shoulders rest comfortably on top and the feet flat on the floor).

Have children "hold up" walls or "push walls down" while waiting in line.

Do pushups with the hands when seated in a chair.

Place your hands on the student's shoulders or head with a safe firm pressure.

Weighted lap pads can be soothing (available in teaching or therapy catalogs).

Weighted neck wraps can also be helpful (available at just about any "Saturday Market"), or make your own by filling a tube of fabric with rice, beans or a mixture of lavender and other calming scents.

Consider alternative forms of seating such as beanbag chairs, molded plastic lawn chairs and inner tubes as well as stability balls.

Have a collection of yoga bands available.

Activities

To develop healthy integration of the PROPRIOCEPTIVE SENSE

- Create an obstacle course that increases in complexity throughout the weeks.
- Have a quiet area that has a weighted blanket, beanbag chair and ear phones.
- Create a kite-flying lesson (have the students make their own by connecting a plastic grocery bag with three feet of string through the two handles of the bag, decorate the kite to individualize).
- Create an eco-friendly community activity around yard work pickup.
- Provide play dough and have the children roll it into snakes.
- Create a woodworking center to calm the student who loves to crash and smash things.
- Have the child make their own water weights – liter size soda bottles filled with water half full, add a little paint, food coloring or small objects such as buttons and sequins. The students can get exercise in carrying them, pushing them, using them as weights, kicking, burying or rolling them.
- Start a game of tug-of-war or develop non-competitive pulling and pushing games.
- Teach a lesson with the stretchy yoga bands such as imitating your movements, or doing the movements to music.

How it Feels

Where you are sitting, pick up all of the belongings that you have with you. Don't put them in a bag or away, just pick up everything, then stand up, move gently around the table counterclockwise, don't forget to push in your chair! Sit down while still holding everything and cross your legs. Now write your name in the air BACKWARDS with your arm fully extended. Keep your arm in the air until you are told to release everything.

After participating in this exercise, what would have helped you to feel more comfortable? Write down a few ideas for adaptations of your own.

_____

_____

_____

_____

"LOOK-ALIKE" CONDITIONS

So many of the characteristics of sensory integration problems can look like other common disorders. Naturally, the symptoms overlap to the point that is difficult to ascertain which behavior is coming from which source. When you look back at the previous examples of the difficulties these children have in school, inattention, hyperactivity, impulsivity, poor social skills, and fidgeting continually come up. How does the classroom teacher decipher what is a sensory integration difficulty and what may be some other disorder such as Attention Deficit Disorder, Oppositional Defiance Disorder, emotional disturbance, a learning disability or some other undiagnosed medical issue? It is not an easy task to identify which behavior is coming from which source, nor is it the teacher's job to "diagnosis" conditions. However, the activities and adaptations that were discussed in the previous sections of this book are helpful for all children.

None of those strategies will HARM any child; it is the matter of finding which intervention works the best with which child. Try everything. Consider yourself a behavior detective; observe patterns of behavior and responses to the interventions. After all, a label that identifies a disorder doesn't help much when you are faced with this child in the classroom on a daily basis. What WILL help is having some practical strategies to try. That being said, I have provided some information for the various kinds of conditions that mimic each other and create challenging behaviors in the classroom. Please don't take the information on the following pages as permission to diagnose such conditions; it is intended to give you an idea of the specific characteristics that are evident in each of the disabilities.

ATTENTION DEFICIT HPERACTIVITY DISORDER

As you well know, Attention Deficit Disorder (ADD) and Attention Deficit Hyperactivity Disorder (ADHD) are behavioral conditions that are primarily exhibited in poor impulse control, lack of inhibition, poor working memory and distractibility and/or inattention. New research indicates that Attention Deficit Disorder can be classified as a multi-sensory processing disorder in which the child is unable to attend to relevant information because of the inefficiency of processing information in the prefrontal cortex (the CEO of the brain). Some children who have been diagnosed as having ADHD and placed on medication may actually have a sensory processing disorder – oops.

You should also consider that there is a difference between inattention and distractibility, one of the characteristics of ADHD. Some kiddos are DISTRACTIBLE because they pay attention TO EVERYTHING in the environment and thus are *over stimulated.* Some kiddos are INATTENTIVE because they pay attention TO NOTHING in the environment long enough to be able to appropriately act on it because they are *under stimulated.* Other kiddos lack the ability to *integrate the relevant information* through their senses into new learning, so they wiggle a LOT to try to ease their discomfort.

Hmmm, now that sounds an awful lot like some OTHER disorder doesn't it?

For our purposes it may help to examine ADHD from a multi-sensory processing deficit angle. Just about any of the ideas for adaptations and activities in this book will be helpful if you can determine if the student is hypo, hyper or integration impaired. On the next few pages are some further considerations for working with students who have the ADHD diagnosis (for better or worse). These ideas specifically address their needs in the classroom.

Approaches that Work Best for Students with ADHD

Selectively ignore minor misbehaviors.

Logical consequences work far better than punishment.

Observe those behaviors that may be coming from a sensory stimulation source. Children who are oversensitive may get hyperactive and volatile, while children who are under sensitive crave stimulation and create it.

Redirect the student with ADHD by using pre-arranged signals and non-verbal cues.

Provide alternative activities when the ADHD student appears upset.

Display desired behaviors on charts and graphs.

Teach the student with ADHD step-by-step behavioral expectations.

Schedule breaks and activities between long periods of academic study.

Select a buddy to help the student with transitions.

Because they have a hard time focusing. . .

1. Develop and maintain a clear focus to the class and lesson.
2. Use highlighters, outlines, and graphic organizers.
3. Keep assignments short.
4. Keep things interesting.
5. Allow for frequent short breaks.
6. Get the student's full attention prior to giving directions.
7. Give them an active role in class projects.

Because they are disorganized . . .

1. Require notebook checks.
2. Have a checklist of things needed for class.
3. Visibly post materials needed for each activity.
4. Keep the classroom organized.
5. Minimize visual clutter.
6. Follow a routine as much as possible.
7. Use planning sheets for long-range projects.
8. Use a daily assignment log.
9. Do unpleasant tasks first.
10. Use file folders and desk organizers.

Because they need more structure, not less . . .

1. Develop and stick to a structured classwide management plan.
2. Make behavioral expectations clear and measurable.
3. Use the management plan consistently.
4. Praise and encourage appropriate behavior 4x more than the inappropriate behavior occurred.
5. Utilize tangible rewards.
6. Deliver lessons in the ADHD student's proximity.
7. Refer to the student in your lecture.

Because they are easily bored . . .

1. Have alternative assignments or projects available and utilize the principles of differentiated learning.
2. Utilize learning centers.
3. Make lessons exciting and stimulating.
4. Use interests of theirs to capture attention.

Because they are conflict seeking for stimulation...
1. Don't yell!
2. Decrease in voice volume when the student's volume increases.
3. Take a break when the situation becomes emotional.
4. Give the student opportunities to escape the stimulation when it becomes too much.
5. Use humor, but not sarcasm.
6. Listen empathetically.
7. Work on the situation only when things are calm.
8. Observe patterns of behavior to reduce or increase stimulation.

To train the student to recognize possible problem situations use. . .
1. Problem solving worksheets
2. Adult conferences
3. Social stories
4. Journal writing
5. Reflection papers
6. Behavior monitoring cards

Autism Spectrum Disorder

We are all aware of the increase that Autism Spectrum Disorder has seen over the last decade. This disorder is now to the point of epidemic proportions in the United States with the latest figures being quoted at 1 in 150 children diagnosed with autism in the United States (1 in 94 in boys). Autism is a complex neurobiological disorder that affects children of all races, ethnicities and social groups. It is considered a developmental disorder that impairs the child's ability to communicate, relate to others and regulate arousal levels. Because the range of autism is wide, it is helpful to look at this disorder on a continuum that includes mild forms of the disorder (Aspergers) to more severe forms with extreme symptoms such as repetitive behaviors, echolalia and a severe inability to relate to others. Because ASD is usually diagnosed by age three, preschool teachers and elementary school teachers will be faced with the challenge of creating workable programs, interventions and strategies for these children in general education as well as special education settings.

Because Autism Spectrum Disorder is associated with difficulties relating to the environment and the presence of challenging behaviors, it is highly likely that the symptoms of sensory integration difficulties are similar with the characteristics of Autism in how the child deals with environmental stressors. The difference in the two disorders is that the child who is diagnosed with Autism has a collection of *other* symptoms that interfere with his learning including: lack of reciprocating social interaction, delays in communication, and unique ways of interacting with objects. These behaviors are in addition to those behaviors brought about by sensory sensitivities.

I like to think of the child who has Autism has having a *multi-sensory sensory processing* deficit that is *one aspect* of his collection of symptoms. If teachers can lessen the environmental stressors for these children through the kinds of strategies discussed in this manual, we will be on the right track for helping to prevent some behaviors from escalating. You may want to experiment with a variety of adaptations as well as

73

activities for children who demonstrate these difficulties from each of the sensory sections of this manual. For most of us working with these children, it is an on-going experiment in finding what works to calm, sooth, stimulate or turn challenging behaviors into productive ones. It will also be very helpful for you to develop an intervention plan after careful analysis in discovering what works for these kiddos (pages 94).

A factor that may differ from the child who has been diagnosed with ASD and the child who has sensory integration difficulties may also be that of cognitive functioning. Children with Autism typically have cognitive deficits, while children with sensory dysfunction do not necessarily demonstrate cognitive delays as a part of the disorder (although sensory integration issues are not exclusive of other disorders, meaning a child may have a cognitive deficit in addition, but not related to the sensory integration issues). I mention this because students who have sensory integration difficulties may be more likely to understand and be helped by cognitive approaches in coping with and compensating for the challenges in their environment than children who are cognitively impaired. Children with more extreme forms of ASD typically respond better to behavior regimes such as Applied Behavior Analysis, "floor time," and Pivotal Response Training.

The similar strategies for working with children who have challenging behaviors whether they are emanating from ASD or sensory dysfunction include the following:

Predictable routine

Creating a sensory sensitive environment

Observing patterns of behavior

Watching for and preventing escalating behaviors

Teaching and warning the child about transitions

Gradually introducing new sensory experiences

Creating activities that will help the child to expand their sensory "comfort zone" through prescribed activities

Sound familiar?

Fetal Alcohol Syndrome and Other Drug Effects

Of the 30,000 toxic substances that can cross the placental barrier, among the worse one for the effect it has on the developing fetus is alcohol. Because alcohol is a depressant (contrary to popular belief at most fraternity parties) and the fetus is expected to grow at a consistent rate throughout the nine months of pregnancy, alcohol can have a devastating effect on the development of the brain and the central nervous system. Fetal Alcohol Syndrome (now considered a spectrum disorder) covers a continuum of effects from mild brain impairment, and learning disabilities (often seen in reading comprehension and math skills) and behavioral issues, to severe mental retardation and crippling skeletal abnormalities.

What is most commonly known about children with Fetal Alcohol Syndrome is that they have unique facial features; wide set eyes, short pug nose, low set ears and smaller head circumference. While these characteristics may be true of the child who has full-blown FAS, this population only accounts for about 7% of the children who are affected by alcohol or drugs. While it is easy to "see" the handicap in these children when they have physical symptoms, so many other children who have Fetal Alcohol Spectrum Disorder go undiagnosed. Their learning problems, immaturity and explosive behaviors are seen as willful disobedience as opposed to having an organic basis.

Children who have been exposed to alcohol or other drugs like methamphetamine, crack cocaine, heroin, barbiturates and amphetamines have varying delays that are based on the effects these drugs have on the central nervous system. One characteristic that most of these substances have in common is the detrimental outcome they have on how these children process sensory stimulation as well as their difficulties with regulation and arousal. Children who have been prenatally exposed to drugs or alcohol display a range of behaviors, from unpredictable, volatile and explosive to seemingly innocuous events. Remember everything you just read about the child with sensory integration problems? Add it all together, times it by two and you have a child with FASD. Remember also that many of these children have lower cognitive functioning; so many cognitive therapies are not very effective with them. Heavy reliance on visuals, predictability in routine, concrete teaching styles, and controlling stimulation in the classroom will be your best bet for making it through the day with these children.

Learning Disabilities

It is estimated that 20% of school-aged children who have learning disabilities or some other condition also have sensory processing disorders. A learning disability as defined by the Individuals With Disabilities Education Act (IDEA 2004) as *"a disorder in one or more of the basic psychological processes involving understanding and using language spoken or written, which manifests itself in an imperfect ability to listen, speak, read, write, spell or do mathematical calculations."* Although, by this definition, sensory integration is not considered a learning disability, children who have sensory integration problems are at a higher risk for learning disabilities because of their sensitivities that interfere with their psychological processes. The child who has a learning disability in one or more subject areas needs specially designed instruction as well as the kinds of adaptations that have been listed in each section of this manual. Considering the source of the any sensory issues that impact the learning disability may be helpful in identifying good adaptations. This is a brief, non-inclusive and VERY simplified chart for analyzing the learning disability in light of possible sensory difficulties.

Learning Disability Category	Possible Sensory Sources
Math Calculation	Visual Tactile Auditory
Reading Comprehension	Auditory
Reading Decoding	Auditory Visual
Oral Language	Auditory Motor Planning
Written Language	Auditory Visual Tactile Vestibular Proprioceptive

4 DOMAINS OF LEARNING DISABILITIES

INPUT

Is the information input correctly, perceived by the senses
and placed in the correct part of the brain for processing?

MEMORY

Can the student remember the information long enough to translate it into the area of the brain that is necessary to integrate it with existing information?

Can the brain integrate new learning with the old learning to make it usable and efficient?

Can the brain integrate two different tasks and areas of the brain to produce one predictable and accurate outcome?

INTEGRATION

Can the brain instruct the body to accurately produce a product to indicate that the learning has adhered?

OUTPUT

HOW IT FEELS

TAKE A SPELLING TEST

ONLY THREE WORDS

1. _____

2. _____

3. _____

JUST A FEW CONDITIONS . . .

Write with your non-dominant hand

The letters must be upside down and backwards

You MUST write in cursive

NO capital letters

Write these words: mad, angry, frustrated

STUDENTS WITH BEHAVIORAL DISORDERS

Ok, here we go. What about those other kiddos in my class who are just being little pills? Isn't there a "Little Pill" category that doesn't have to do with the sensory sensitivity stuff or other disorders? Do I have to make all sorts of accommodations for those students even when they are choosing to act that way? Wouldn't that be encouraging the Little Pill if I make too many accommodations and adaptations when what they really want is to get out of doing the work or they just want attention? Good questions. And I can decisively say to that concern that the answer is …yes and no.

Some children have behavioral disorders that can fall into the category of "willful disobedience" and can make life for teachers a living hell. Here are some fun facts to know and tell about those kiddos:

Oppositional Defiance Disorder is a behavioral disorder of people who are negativistic, hostile, defiant, contrary and "chronically uncooperative." Although Oppositional Defiance Disorder has been called many different things (Explosive Personality Disorder, Behavior Disorder, Adaptive Behavior Disorder and Anti-Social Disorder) one thing is certain, these students pose significant challenges to the classroom teacher. Students who have been diagnosed with Oppositional Defiance Disorder display many of the following common behavioral patterns: aggressive behaviors, temper tantrums, failure to respect other's property, defiance, refusal to comply with directives and violent behaviors. All students can be oppositional and defiant at times, but for the child who has been diagnosed with this behavioral condition, it is important that teachers and school staff have some extra tools in their toolbox of strategies.

Remember how we established earlier that all behavior is an attempt to communicate something? My first suggestion is that you consider the purpose of the behavior (BTW you don't get to say here, "The purpose of the child's behavior is to make my life a living hell" - that doesn't count).

Looking at those purposes of behavior may help you to determine some environmental things that you can do to help prevent the problem or reduce the intensity, duration and frequency of the behaviors from occurring. Then you apply the ideas about motivation of behaviors and ask yourself if you have tried these important strategies:

1. Implemented and CONSISTENLY used a structured classwide behavioral management system with a well-developed hierarchy of consequences for misbehaviors.

2. Communicated with parents and administration regarding the management system so that you can count on their support.

3. Employed a consistent delivery of consequences with each and every infraction.

4. Provided opportunities for rewards when the child demonstrated appropriate and pro-social behaviors.

5. Made a conscious effort to avoided power struggles.

6. Enlisted the support of your supervisors.

7. Are fully aware of and have implemented the school-wide discipline policy.

8. Followed the proper channels for reporting.

9. Documented everything.

By the way, *I* believe that you did all that stuff. But I will warn you now that when you refer a student to the special education department because you need more help or testing or a program for him, those folks are gonna ask you what you did, how long you tried it and how it worked. The fancy name for this is "Response to Intervention." You might as well be prepared for that. So, document everything that you did with this student prior to going to the special education staff. This way you are not asked to "try some things" first (which you and I know you ALREADY DID) and postpone getting the help this child needs.

Ok, so you did all of that, here are some more ideas for working with the student with oppositional behaviors...

Because they "lock up" cognitively when pushed to comply:

1. Give options - when to do something and how to do it.

2. Distract them for a while to break the negative loop.

3. State your expectations clearly and briefly, one time.

4. Walk away.

5. Come back to the issue later.

6. Avoid power struggles - they will always win.

7. Redirect.

Because they automatically say "NO":

1. Suggest that they hear you out before they say no.

2. Be brief and clear.

3. Say, "You probably wouldn't want to do this but...."

4. Use reverse psychology or paradoxical requests.

5. Have them write out options.

6. Build rapport.

Because they misbehave:

1. Deal with misbehavior quickly, firmly and unemotionally.

2. Chose your battles.

3. Watch for signs of escalation.

4. Provide logical consequences offered as a choice.

5. Set the standard of "No arguing with adults."

6. Do not give in.

Because there are chemical changes in the brain:

1. Be aware of nutritional issues– high carbohydrates and l-tryptophan.

2. Exercise can help – pushing, pulling or lifting heavy objects.

3. Suggest the student drink plenty of water.

4. Avoid sudden changes and surprises.

Other Approaches that Work for Students with Behavior Disorders

1. **Say a prayer.**

2. **Use redirection when attempting to change undesired behavior.**
    Instead of saying, *"SIT DOWN!"* say, *"Aya, can you look at your schedule to see what you should be doing next?"* Use the "back door approach" or reverse psychology versus correction.

3. **Ask questions that provide acceptable alternatives when attempting to encourage positive behaviors.**
    "Jose, which would you rather work on at this time, math or social studies?"

4. **Help with time management.**
    "Inga, how can I help you to get this accomplished by lunch time so you can go out to play?" Use a talking clock or put the schedule on the board.

5. **Avoid surprises and unexpected changes.**
    "Today, at 9:00, we will be having a guest speaker instead of going to PE."

6. **Watch for initial signs that the student is becoming upset.**
    "Billy, how are you doing? Would you like some time-in?"

7. **Build relationships with students that are based on trust and respect.** *"You seem quiet today, how are you doing, Annica?"*

8. **Adjust the student's academic schedule when it is obvious they are having a difficult day or are about ready to explode** *"Why don't you work on something else for awhile?"*

9. **Adjust academic challenges to meet the ability levels of this student.**
    "Instead of doing them all, would you like to do the odd or the even numbered problems?"

10. **Have practiced procedures for removal of the student away from the classroom.** *Most behaviorally disordered students inevitably will need to be removed from the class at some point. Have procedures for safe and orderly removal from the classroom.*

Disorder	Purpose of Bx	Pivotal Issue	Academics	Strategies	Effective Discipline	Best Practice	Goal
Sensory Processing Dysfunction	Stimulation or escape misinterpretation	Environment and teacher response	Dependent on environmental stressors	Environmental modifications Activities to build tolerance Predictability	Prevent Time In Time Out	Prevent Observe Patterns Bx Adaptations	For the child to learn to self-regulate in the face of environmental stressors
Autism Spectrum Disorder	Stimulation Escape Desire	Environment people and activity	Splinter skills Environmentally dependent	Picture schedules Environmental	Prevent Rewards Time out	Consistency Concrete Visual	To develop an individual cache of skills for maximum independence
Fetal Alcohol Syndrome Disorder	Developmental Cognitive deficit	Environment Memory Communication	Splinter skills Avg. reading, poor comp, math and lang.	Visuals Routine Environmental Multi-modality	Redirect Clear limits Bx Mod	Visual modify expectations	To develop and use effective daily living skills consistently
Attention Deficit Hyperactivity Disorder	Impulsivity Lacking in inhibition Performance deficit	Maintenance of attention	Attention span distractibility interferes with academics	Organization STAR Movement	General plan monitoring systems, charts	Stimulate and organize	To think before acting
Learning Disability	Frustration Avoidance Inability Processing	Teaching style	Strengths and weaknesses due to processing deficits	SDI, Learning styles Scaffolding learning	General plan	Multi-modality, persistence Creative	To learn skills by compensating for weaknesses by building on strengths
Behavior Disorder CD; ODD	Control/ego; Avoidance of the unknown	Teacher response style	Average or refusals; Resistant to get started by average	Matter of fact Consistent Paradoxical responses	Level systems Removal of privileges	Avoid power struggles Paradoxical approaches	Compliance with authority Utilize pro-social behaviors to meet needs.
Emotional Disturbance	Skill deficit	Identifying issues and new skills	Dependent on self-esteem behavioral issues	Flexibility Nurturance Limit setting	Clear boundaries Positives	Counsel Instruct	For the child to recognize triggers & respond appropriately

Emotional overlays

When you have a sensory integration disorder, the world can be a crazy, unpredictable and even frightening place. It is not unlikely that after dealing with painful and anxiety-producing experiences 24/7 that no one else seems to understand, at some point you are going to start to feel bad about yourself, "different" or just plain angry and frustrated.

The child who is sensory sensitive may display the following emotional characteristics:

Easily frustrated
Becomes volatile for no apparent reason
Mood swings
Gives up quickly
Reluctant to try new activities
Has a low tolerance for stressful situations
Has low self-esteem
Becomes irritable and/or withdraws around others
Has poor peer relations or difficulty making friends
Becomes very rigid or reluctant in trying new activities
Avoids participation in sensory-laden activities
Becomes timid in unfamiliar situations
Often says, "I can't do that" before even trying
Does the same activities over and over again that are "sensory safe"
Is physically tired at the end of the day
Shows obsessive-compulsive behaviors
Is school or socially phobic
Becomes depressed
Diagnosed with Generalized Anxiety Disorder
Consistently refuses
Demonstrates unpredictable aggression
Has panic attacks
Depersonalizes and disassociates behaviors
Becomes addicted to substances
Suicidal thoughts, talk or ideation

Thinking Outside the Box

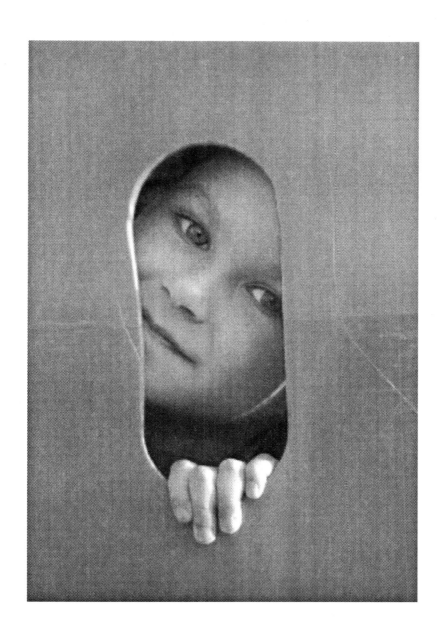

SCHEDULING

Scheduling and routines encourage predictability. Predictability can lessen the disruptions, and manage the sensory input. For children with sensory integration issues, providing them with predictable routines is necessary to manage the behaviors that emanate from sensory overload or integration difficulties as well as problems caused by under stimulation.

Starting the day is critical to optimal performance and eliminating unnecessary stimulation that precedes problematic behavior. Here are some ideas for scheduling and establishing routines:

Develop and utilize hello and goodbye rituals.

Start each day with a circle time that explains the schedule for the day and addresses possible changes, interruptions or current issues.

Organize cubbies so that children have a consistent place to keep their things.

Post the schedule for the day on the board and refer to it often.

Give the child an individual copy of the schedule so that they can refer to it and check it off as activities or subjects are completed.

Laminate a copy of a consistent schedule and have the child check off the activities with a dry erase marker.

Develop and utilize individual picture schedules.

Use transitional objects for young children (the child carries something from a place that they left into the new place so that they feel the safe connection between places).

Use timers and warnings for transitions to new activities.

Teach the schedule, teach changes in routine, and warn about changes.

Allow for extra time for transitions.

Intersperse quiet activities with more active lessons.

Use puppets to explain activities, transitions and schedules.

Use music to transition to different activities.

Use hand signals to indicate changes or transitions

Josie's Picture Schedule

Class meeting

done

Math

done

Reading

done

Recess

done

Art

done

Lunch

done

Have each picture seen here on cards stuck to the chart by Velcro, the child takes off the picture and puts it in the "done pocket" turned backwards which signals the end of the activity.

Effective Discipline Techniques

While it is important to create an environment to prevent sensory-induced behaviors from occurring or escalating into full-blown meltdowns, it is also important to have a predictable discipline style and student management plan that creates a safe environment for all kids. Although many of these children's behaviors may emanate from their sensory processing issues, it is important to remember that kids are still kids. All children test the boundaries, wake-up on the wrong side of the bed or can be oppositional or aggressive at times. Sensory processing issues do not negate the need for a clear discipline plan in the classroom that allows all members to be clear about the expectations and consequences as well as get positive recognition for performing the expectations. Since predictability is so important for children with sensory issues, they probably need the clear management plan practiced consistently even more than the other children. Teachers should be aware that the majority of the difficult behaviors are born out of deep frustration, are protective (fight or flight reactions) or are symptomatic of the disorder. For the typical child, power struggles may result in behavior change or ceasing if the adult persists (i.e., the adult eventually wins). For the teacher who engages in power struggles with a child who has sensory problems, everyone loses.

A CLASSROOM MANAGEMENT PLAN SHOULD:

Clearly define, teach, and rehearse classroom expectations.

Be visibly posted with picture or verbal descriptions.

State expectations in the positive; e.g., "walking feet" instead of "don't run."

List no more than five expectations (aka, rules), no fewer than three.

Also listed on the plan should be a series of consequences in a hierarchy for dealing with minor to serious infractions.

List ways that children will be positively recognized for behaving appropriately.

Reward appropriate behavior with approval and positives.

If you don't have a management plan like this, do it immediately and make it an integral part of your classroom.

Some Other Considerations

SET LIMITS AND BE FIRM ABOUT THE LIMITS

USE THE MANAGEMENT PLAN CONSISTENTLY

NEVER DISCIPLINE A SENSORY-SEEKER BY TAKING AWAY RECESS OR OTHER MOVEMENT OPPORUNTITIES

TIME IN

Observing patterns of behavior so that the child can be alerted as to when he is starting to escalate and can make a choice to "take a breather".

TIME OUT

An established quiet area that is set aside for the purpose of calming oneself. Have an hourglass (rather than a ticking clock) and when the time in the hourglass is up, the child may leave time out.

COACHING THE CHILD TO DEEP BREATHE

Teach the child relaxation strategies prior to the moment when they need it to calm their behavior. Practice breathing in for three counts holding for three counts and releasing for three counts. I taught my students how to count by saying, "One hippopotamus in a tutu, two hippopotamus in a tutu" (it still makes me smile to remember their serious little faces concentrating on the silly words). Use a visual signal or a special word to remind them to use it after the skill has been well learned and practiced.

OBSERVE THE PATTERNS OF BEHAVIOR

You know the saying, "an ounce of prevention is worth a pound of cure." Watch for things that you know set off behavior. Redirecting, guiding the child toward a stimulation-free area or other techniques learned in this manual will be important.

It may be that the behavior gets predictably worse during certain times of the day, during certain activities, around certain people, or in certain rooms. Be a "behavior detective" in determining what may be escalating the behavior and use good prevention techniques.

SEPARATE THE CHILD FROM THE BEHAVIOR

It is ok to say, "I feel frustrated" to the child. Much better than to say, "You are a little twerp, just wait until I call your mother."

IF BEHAVIOR BECOMES COMPLETELY OUT OF CONTROL

Remove the child to a prearranged quiet area outside of the classroom.

Establish a trusted contact person who can retrieve the child and guide them to the area.

Establish a team of people to intervene if the student's behavior becomes violent.

Remove the class if necessary.

Follow up with consequences long after the behavior has completely calmed.

NEVER USE RESTRAINT HOLDS UNLESS YOU HAVE BEEN TRAINED AND CERTIFIED, AND EVEN THEN WITH GREAT CAUTION.

Ideas for Helping Children to Regulate Their Own Behaviors in the Classroom

It is the teacher's job to help the sensory-sensitive child find the skills necessary to self-regulate when stimulation gets to be overwhelming. As with the adults who work with them, these children will be better off if they learn to recognize the precursors to their behaviors and do prevention strategies that work for them.

Teach the children these coping strategies and be flexible when they need to use them:

Excuse yourself to find some privacy

Go to a quiet area away from people and other distractions

Put on head phones

Listen to music

Breathe deeply

Interlock your hands and place them on the crown of your head to calm your central nervous system

Walk briskly

Distract yourself

Drink water

Talk the situation over with an adult you trust

Do yoga stretches

Listen to a progressive relaxation tape

A Couple of Programs

The RELAX Program is a good one for helping children to identify their stressors and how it feels in their bodies. It can help the child to identify where the stressors are in their bodies by coloring on a handout with a body shape on it. It is available from Ready, Set, RELAX: A Research Based Program for Relaxation, Learning and Self-Esteem for Children.

The ALERT Program for Self Regulation "How Does Your Engine Run?" has the following ideas to help teach children how to recognize sensory sensitivities and arousal states that relate to attention, behavior and learning. It uses the metaphor of a car engine and how quickly it is running or how slowly. One lesson helps them to identify their own coping devices:

When my engine is too fast	I feel	It helps to do these things
When my engine is running too slow	I feel	It helps to do these things

Developing a Plan to Stop EXPLOSIVE BEHAVIORS

Once we figure out that there are some behavioral issues that may be stemming from sensory sensitivities and we have tried a number of adaptation strategies, but things STILL aren't working as well as we had planned, it may be time to bring in the BIG GUNS. That is, to develop a more specific individualized behavior plan for a kiddo so that everyone who works with him or her can be on the same page. When determining children for behavioral interventions it is wise to consider how you can lessen the intensity, duration and frequency of the behavior and keep it from escalating from a minor misbehavior into a major misbehavior.

The Four W's

In order to determine the exact nature, severity, frequency and duration of the problem, it is necessary to do a little investigative work. Use this page to promote discussion among those who work with the child who demonstrates the challenging behaviors.

Define the Behavior
What is the behavior that we are most concerned about?

Where does this behavior occur?

With **whom** does it occur?

When does the behavior occur?

What is happening **before** the behavior occurs?

What is happening **right after** the behavior occurs?

Empty Spaces

Just as it is important to determine the nature of troublesome behaviors, it can be a very valuable exercise to examine the "empty spaces" of when, where, who, and what is happening when the behaviors NEVER (or rarely) occur. If we can determine when the child is behaving appropriately, calmly, or at a manageable arousal level, it is possible that we can replicate the same circumstances to prevent the behaviors from occurring at all. Use this page to promote discussion regarding the possibilities for replication.

Where does this behavior NOT occur?

With **whom** does it NOT occur?

When do the behaviors NOT occur?

What is NOT happening **before** the behavior occurs?

What is NOT happening **right after** the behavior occurs?

How could the characteristics of this situation be replicated?

On the next page you get to put everything together that you have collected in your data gathering. Here is a format for developing a consistent plan for everyone to follow who works with this student. . .

Intervention Plan

1. Define the Problem
   Description of the Problem Behavior

2. Gather Information: *The behavior is happening...*
   With these people:

   During this activity:

   During this time of day:

   In this location:

3. Develop a Theory
   What do you believe is the purpose of the behavior?

   ☐ Attention   ☐ Desire
   ☐ Stimulation   ☐ Revenge
   ☐ Escape   ☐ Biological
                        ☐ Avoidance

4. Identify the Replacement Behavior
   What do you want the child to do instead that would get his needs met in an appropriate manner?

5. Make a plan
   Prevent
   What environmental adaptations will be made to reduce the incidences?

   Teach
   What new replacement behavior or skill will be taught to the student so that he can get his needs and wants met appropriately?

   Cues
   Verbal   _____
   Visual   _____
   Gestures _____

6. Use the Plan
   Behaviors tracked and documented

   ☐ Home-school communication book   ☐ Time In
   ☐ Response cost   ☐ Behavior Chart
   ☐ Time out   ☐ Behavior Log

7. Evaluate the Plan   Beginning date _____   Continue _____
                           Ending date _____   Modify _____
                           All adults trained _____ Terminate _____
                                                      Different Behavior _____

Signatures

_____   _____

_____   _____

Student Name: _Jaleshia_   **Date:**   April 1

1. Current Problem

Jaleshia is aggressive and oppositional whenever the class lines up. She hits others, is defiant and argumentative and makes rude comments to others.

2. Data

People: *Peers, the teacher, and any adult who is escorting the class to the cafeteria*
Activities: *Lining up and walking down the hall*
Time of day: *Just before lunch*
Location: *Classroom, hallway and cafeteria*

3. Theory: *Because the behavior only occurs while going to the cafeteria, in the classroom, lining up and walking to the cafeteria, the team is hypothesizing that the cause of her behavior is sensory induced by the smells and her desire to avoid them.*

☐ Attention	☐ Desire
☐ Stimulation	☐ Revenge
☐ Escape	☑ Biological
	☑ Avoidance

4. Replacement Behavior

Jaleshia will walk down the hall to the cafeteria, follow the adult's directions and use respectful language while keeping her hands, feet and objects to herself.

5. Plan

<u>Prevention</u>
Warn Jaleshia about the schedule and that lunchtime is approaching.
Designate that she will be the permanent line leader.
She will hold the hand of the adult.
She will have a smelly sticker or canister of her favorite smell with her as she walks down the hall.

<u>Teach</u>
Jaleshia will use the following words to indicate that she is becoming over stimulated or having difficulty with the stimulation, "I need a breather." Or she will put her finger underneath her nose.
When she says or does this she will be directed to smell her favorite smell and deep breathe.
Jaleshia will investigate the scents she finds soothing through activities such as Smello and Smash and Smell.
She will make her own canister of her favorite smell to use as a transitional object to the cafeteria.
Cues, visual, gestures" <u>Put your finger underneath your nose so Jaleshia can mimic</u>
Verbal "<u>Take a Breather</u>" _____

5. Implementation

☐ Home-school communication book	☑ Time In
☑ Response cost	☐ Behavior Chart
☑ Time out	☐ Behavior

Beginning date: April 1   Ending date: May 25   All adults trained _____

6. Evaluate   Continue   Modify   Terminate   New Behavior

Signatures

_____   _____
_____   _____

Quick and Dirty Reference Guide for Sensory Integration Issues

Sensory System	Affected by	Strategies to try
Visual Processing	Light/dark Visual Clutter	Avoid hanging things from the ceiling Remove excess on the walls and shelves Visual boundaries Verbally define and decribe Carpet squares Idividual desks Natural lighting Color overlays Replace florescent bulbs with full spectrum Highly organized room Everything has a place Visual schedules Opaque containers rather than clear
Auditory Processing	Sound and Noise	Headphones Take walks outside for a break White noise machine Give specific, one step directions Small groups Read the directions All adequate time to answer Speak slowly Visual cue to call on Give question, delay, call on first

Sensory System	Affected by	Strategies to try
Proprioceptive	Very tactile Unaware of personal space Clumsy Difficulty motor planning	Mini-trampoline Bear hug to self Use a firm touch rather than light Warn child before touching Gradual intro to tactile activities Personal space lessons Push or carry heavy objects Social stories Weghted blankets and vests
Vestibular	Motion Movement in Space	Adequate time on the playground Music and movement Obstacle course Rocking chairs
Multi-sensory	Attention. Concentration Can't organize body	Make two lines instead of one long one Seated near the teacher at floor time Seated at the end of the table at snack Fidgets during circle or lecture times Intersperse active times with quiet times Prolong and emphasize transition times Frequent breaks Prevention

Other Nifty Ideas

Mandalas

Mandalas have been known throughout history to calm and create inner peace. For children who are having trouble focusing coloring a mandala can be a relaxing activity or can help them to center or focus. They are designs that are to be colored in. Research indicates that coloring from the outside toward the center can help someone to focus, and coloring from the inside to the outside can help to calm. You can download great ideas from www.mandali.com. It is a perfect activity for anyone who wants to relax, or quiet him or herself. Mandalas can also be found in Everyone's Mandala Coloring Book Vol 1, 2 or 3. and ordered from Amazon.com.

SMELLO

SMELLO

(Use the labels from food containers for the pictures.)

A copy to develop your own

Things that smell GOOD
Things that smell BAD

Collect objects for smelling, have the student draw smiley or frowny faces in the circles. Let them identify which smells are pleasant for them or not by completing this sheet. You can modify this sheet for taste.

103

Writing Paper

KINDERGARTEN

FIRST THROUGH SIXTH

Directionality Paper

Sentence and Word Windows

Simply cut out a window from a piece of paper that isolates one sentence or one word at a time so that there is a significant amount of white space around visual stimuli. (also available at most office supply stores are sentence highlighter strips that have the window concept using tinted plastic that overlays onto the printed material).

Configuration Cues

This is the activity of having the student draw a box around words to help them identify the shape of the words, thus tapping into the visual memory rather than just phonemic memory.

Organization

To help children to organize papers that need to be left at home and those that need to be returned to school, use a folder with a front pocket and a back pocket. On the left side, have the child draw around their left hand and write "LEFT AT HOME." On the right side, have the child draw around their right hand and write "BRING RIGHT BACK." This will not only suffice as an organization device but uses a mnemonic device to enhance memory AND teaches directionality.

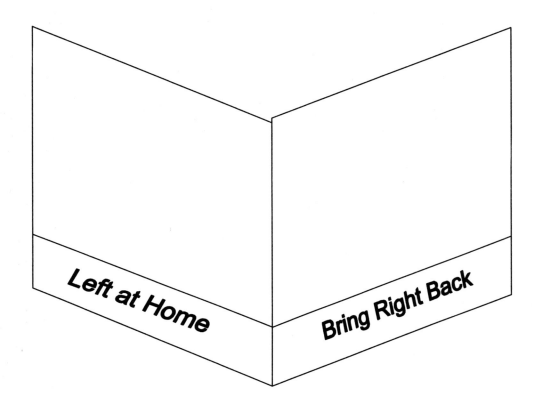

Educational Kinesiology Brain Gym®

Educational Kinesiology (Edu-K for short), also known Brain Gym movements, can help children to become more focused and calm.

The philosophy behind this program is that the human brain functions in terms of three dimensions: laterality, focus, and centering. Successful brain function requires efficient connections across the neural pathways located throughout the brain. Stress inhibits these connections, while the Brain Gym movements stimulate a flow of information along these networks, restoring the innate ability to learn and function with curiosity and joy.

Brain Gym provides movement activities for classroom teachers that are easy to do, can be interspersed between other activities, and indicate documented improvements in learning, vision, memory, expression and movement abilities, in both young people and adults. In the classroom, teachers typically report improvements in attitude, attention, homework, behavior, and academic performance for the entire class. If you are interested in Brain Gym exercises, you may want to check it out at www.braingym.com.

Resources

Books

Anderson, Elizabeth and Pauline Emmons. Unlocking the Mysteries of Sensory Dysfunction. Future Horizons, Inc. Arlington, TX 76013.

Bogashina, Olga. Sensory Perceptual Issues in Autism and Asperberger Syndrome. Jessica Kingsley Publishers. 2003.

Davis, Diane. Reaching Out to Children with FAS/FAE. A Handbook for Teachers, Counselors and Parents who work with Children Affected by Fetal Alcohol Syndrome and Effects. The Center for Applied Research in Education 1994.

Greenspan, Stanley. The Challenging Child (1995).

Heller, Sharon PhD. Too Loud Too Bright Too Fast Too Tight: What to Do If You Are Sensory Defensive in an Over Stimulating World. Quill 2002.

Legge, Brenda.   Can't Eat Won't Eat. Dietary Difficulties and Autism Spectrum Disorder. Jessica Kingsley Publishers, 2002.

Koomar, Jane. Answers to Questions Teachers Ask About Sensory Integration. Sensory Resources, Watertown, MA. October 2005.

Kranowitz, Stock Carol MA. The Out of Sync Child. Berkley Publishing Company 2005.

Kranowitz, Stock Carol MA. The Out of Sync Child Has Fun: Activities for Kids with Sensory Integration Dysfunction. Berkeley Publishing Company, 2005.

Phillips, Kathryn. Successful Strategies for Working with Challenging Elementary Students. Total Behavior Management. www.totalbehaviormanagement.com
 2006.

Smith, Karen A, and Karen R. Grouze. The Sensory Sensitive Child: Practical Solutions for Out of Bounds Behavior. Harper Collins Publisher 2004.

Young Exceptional Children Volume 8 No.1 "Meeting the Sensory Needs of Young Children in Classrooms", 2006.

Villarreal, Sylvia Fernandez MD et al.   Handle with Care: Helping Children Prenatally Exposed to Drugs and Alcohol. ETR Associates, Santa Cruz California 1991.

Websites

Sensory Integration International. www.sensoryint.com

Incredible Horizons. www.incrediblehorizons.com/sensoryintergration

Sensory Processing Disorders Foundation www.kidpower.com

www.sensorysmarts.com

www.specialkidszobne.com

www.otawatertown.com

www.totalbehaviormanagement.com

Programs

How Does your Engine Run? The Alert Program for Self-Regulation

Ready Set, RELAX: A Research Based Program for Relaxation, Learning and Self-Esteem for Children.

Materials

www.babybumblebee.com

www.weightedbalnket.net

www.specialneedstoys.com

www.ideatrainingcenter.com

www.discoverytoolsandworkshops.com

mbmagicboards@comcast.net

www.mandali.com

Assessing Behavior in Children

A Practical System for
Solving Challenging Behaviors
In Early Childhood Settings

$26.95 $7.00 shipping and handling
ISBN 0-9776218-0-4

Dealing with Difficult Parents
A Survival Guide for Teachers

$26.95 $7.00 shipping and handling
ISBN 0-9776218-1-2

The Ultimate Playground Guide
Solving Common Discipline
Problems k–6

$26.95 $7.00 shipping and handling
ISBN 0-9776218-1-2

NEW!

Successful Strategies
for working with
Challenging
Elementary Students

Kathryn P. Phillips M.A

Teachers spend eighty percent of their time with twenty percent of their students! It is the challenging student that gets our attention, but many teachers use ineffective strategies with the challenging child that can actually escalate misbehaviors unnecessarily. In this highly sought manual, you will find dozens of strategies for dealing effectively with challenging elementary children. Included are reproducibles for travel cards, behavior essays, point systems, behavior charts, as well as the best practices for establishing behavior intervention plans and alternative learning environments simply and immediately. You CAN"T do without this book!

$26.95 $7.00 shipping and handling
ISBN 0-9776218-4-7